How Do I Stay Safe From Online Predators?

Tricia Yearling

How Do I Stay Safe From Online Predators?

Tricia Yearling

Enslow Publishing
101 W. 23rd Street
Suite 240
New York, NY 10011
USA

enslow.com

Words to Know

chat room—An online place where people can type messages to each other.

identity—The traits that make people who they are.

online profile—Information about himself or herself that a person enters to be stored on a Web site.

predator—A person who tries to control or harm another person.

prey—A person who is hunted for and possibly harmed by another person.

World Wide Web—A network of connected Web sites.

Contents

Stranger Danger

If you play games online, do research for school, or watch YouTube videos, you use the Internet. The Internet is like a giant park. You can play games there. You can discover many interesting things. You can even meet up with friends. However, like in any public place, you may meet people you don't know. It's important to take steps to be safe.

When you go to a park, you watch out for strangers. On the Internet, you need to watch out

The key to protecting yourself online is to keep your personal information private.

for online **predators**. These people use the Internet to try to meet children. They try to become friends with kids and ask them to do things that kids should not do. Knowing how to deal with online predators will help you stay safe while you are having fun online.

Who Are You?

In a park or any other public place, you can see a stranger. You can look at a person's face and clothing and hear his or her voice. This is not possible to do when you are online. People can make up their **identities** online. They can pick

When you go to a public beach, you can see everyone around you. On the Internet, people can lie about who they really are.

new names. They can lie about their ages and where they live. They can even use someone else's picture as their own.

Unless you are chatting with someone you know in person, you cannot know for sure whom you are talking to online. Online predators often pretend to be people they are not. They may even pretend to be other kids.

Where Predators Hunt

Many kids spend time online in **chat rooms** or playing online games. Online predators try to meet kids in these places.

They read the chats kids are having, and then send private messages to kids they think will

SAFETY TIP! Chat only with people you know in person.

Chat rooms are fun places to talk about things you are interested in. However, you must watch out for online predators.

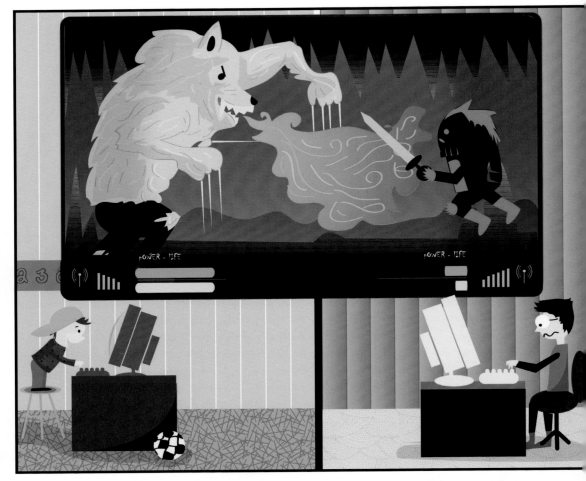

Gamers from all over the world may play online games together. Do not answer messages from players you do not know. They may just be pretending to be kids to try to talk to you.

respond. Online predators also leave notes for people on Web sites and send messages by e-mail. Predators will sometimes join online games where players are talking to each other and reach out to other players.

The first messages from a predator may sound like they are from a friend. They may ask, "What's up?" Then they may ask for your real name or age. If you receive messages like these from someone you don't know, do not respond to them. These are messages from strangers. Never answer questions from a stranger. Do not even write back.

SAFETY TIP!

Open messages only from people you know.

Dealing With an Online Predator

Online predators try to become familiar with their **prey** and earn their trust. They may reach out to you several times over many weeks. A predator may ask if he can send you pictures. He may also want you to send pictures of yourself. He may offer to send you presents. He will try to get more information from you about yourself, your family, or your friends. Some predators may even ask you to do things that make you feel uncomfortable. Getting messages from an

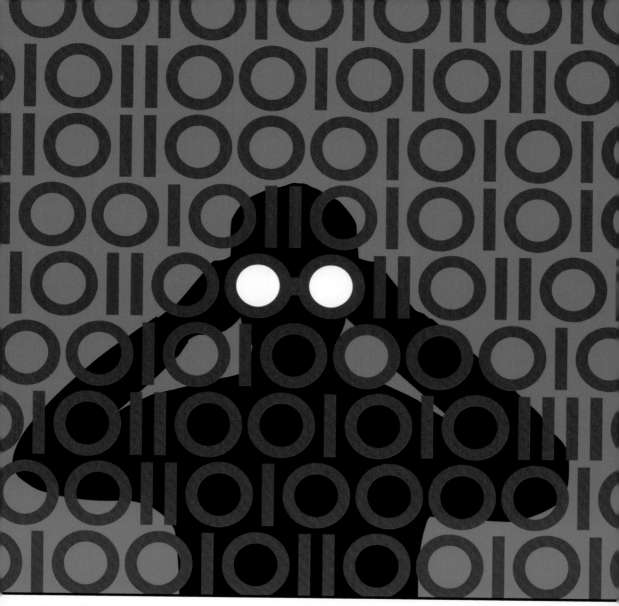

An online predator may seem nice at first. He or she may act like a friend or try to give you gifts. But these are just tricks to earn your trust. Do not accept anything from an online predator.

Being bothered by an online predator can make you feel angry, sad, scared, or all of these things.

SAFETY TIP!

Never give out your phone number or call a number that was given to you by someone you met online.

online predator can be very scary and upsetting. However, you can take control of the situation.

Taking Action

It is important for you to know that if a predator sends you messages, it is not your fault. Whether the message comes in a chat room, by e-mail, or while you are playing a game, you have not done anything wrong. It is the predator who is wrong. You are also not alone. Predators try to reach out to many people. Do not feel embarrassed or trapped. With a little help, you can take control and put a stop to the messages and the predator.

The first thing to do if a predator sends you messages is to tell a parent, guardian, or trusted teacher. Go online with the person you tell and show him or her the messages that you received. Tell the adult everything that happened. Together you can make a plan to keep the predator from bothering you.

Breaking the Law

Preying on people online is against the law. Online predators are criminals. If someone asks you to do something that does not seem right or sends you inappropriate pictures or movies, tell

If an online predator contacts you, he or she is breaking the law. The police can help stop the predator from contacting you.

Tell an adult if you receive disturbing messages, pictures, or videos from a stranger online. He or she can then report it to the police.

SAFETY TIP!

If someone online tells you something that makes you feel uncomfortable, it is probably inappropriate. Tell an adult right away.

an adult who can contact the police. You may feel uncomfortable and scared, and that is okay. Remember that the predator is the person who did something wrong, not you. The police know how to deal with predators and can help you.

If you have messages, pictures, or movies that a predator has sent you, tell the police about all of them. Do not print any of these things. Instead, ask the police what you should do with them.

Catching the Predator

When you report an online predator to the police, they will ask you questions about the messages you received. They may also ask to check your computer. This will let them take a good look at the messages themselves.

There are many ways police officers chase online predators. They examine the messages that kids report having received. The police may set up "sting operations" in which officers pretend to be kids and go into chat rooms or play online games. The officers may even set up real-life meetings with predators. When the predators show up, the police officers arrest them.

SAFETY TIP!

By reporting a predator's behavior, you can help to prevent other kids from being approached.

The police want to help and protect people from predators.

Staying Safe Online

There are easy ways to protect yourself from being approached by an online predator. Don't tell anyone online your real name, age, or where you live. Don't use this information in your **online profile** either. Also do not share facts such as your school name, team names, phone number, or e-mail address. These are all ways a predator can reach you.

Stay away from Web sites with chat rooms that are not watched over by adults. Do not post

Being careful and following some simple rules will help keep you safe from online predators.

pictures of yourself online. Share your instant-messaging contact or e-mail address only with your family and very best friends.

Keep It Online

Before talking to people online, talk with your parents or guardian. Come up with a list of safety rules for what you can do online. Visit some Web sites together and choose the ones that are right for you. One rule every person must follow is that you will never agree to meet in person someone whom you met online.

It is ok to take pictures of yourself and your friends, but do not post them online. Make sure your friends do not post pictures of you either.

Being online is like riding a bike around your neighborhood. You need to take the steps necessary to stay safe in a public place.

The **World Wide Web** is a public place. You will encounter people you do not know there, and you must be careful around them. This does not mean you have to be scared. It just means that you have to take the right steps to make sure you are safe when you are online.

SAFETY TIP!

Talk to a trusted adult before visiting sites that let you talk to strangers.

Learn More

Books

Cosson, M. J. *The Smart Kid's Guide to Using the Internet.* North Mankato, Minn.: The Child's World, 2014.

DiOrio, Rana. *What Does It Mean to Be Safe?* San Francisco, Calif.: Little Pickle Press, 2011.

Rustad, Martha E. H. *Learning About Privacy*. Mankato, Minn.: Capstone Press, 2015.

Web Sites

commonsensemedia.org/privacy-and-internet-safety

Provides Internet safety tips.

privacy.getnetwise.org/sharing/tips/passwords

Gives tips on password safety.

netsmartz.org/NetSmartzKids/PasswordRap

Advice for creating a strong password.

Index

Published in 2016 by Enslow Publishing, LLC.
101 W. 23rd Street, Suite 240, New York, NY 10011

Library of Congress Cataloging-in-Publication Data
Yearling, Tricia.
 How do I stay safe from online predators? / Tricia Yearling.
    pages cm.— (Online smarts)
 Includes bibliographical references and index.
 Summary: "Discusses how kids can protect themselves from online predators"—Provided by publisher.
 ISBN 978-0-7660-6854-4 (library binding)
 ISBN 978-0-7660-6853-7 (pbk.)
 ISBN 978-0-7660-6974-9 (6-pack)
 1. Online sexual predators—Juvenile literature. 2. Internet—Security measures—Juvenile literature. I. Title.
 HV6773.15.O58Y43 2015
 025.042028'9—dc23

                    2015007455

Printed in the United States of America

To Our Readers: We have done our best to make sure all Web sites in this book were active and appropriate when we went to press. However, the author and the publisher have no control over and assume no liability for the material available on those Web sites or on any Web sites they may link to. Any comments or suggestions can be sent by e-mail to customerservice@enslow.com.

Photo Credits: Alexandra Grablews/The Image Bank/Getty Images, p. 25; Alistair Berg/Digitial Vision/Getty Images, p. 27; BJI/Blue Jean Images/Getty Images, p. 5; Elena Kalistratova/iStock/Thinkstock (chapter opener and front and back matter); Fanatic Studio/Getty Images, p. 12; junpinzon/Shutterstock.com, p. 16; kali9/E+/Getty Images, p. 20; Monkey Business Images/Shutterstock.com (group of kids), p. 3; NigelSpiers/Shutterstock.com, p. 9; Pascal Broze/ONOKY/Getty Images, p. 11; Patrick George/Ikon Images/Getty Images, p. 15; Purestock/Thinkstock (series logo), p. 3; Rafe Swan/Cultura/Getty Images, p. 19; Shouoshu/iStock/Thinkstock (digital background), p. 3; Rob Marmion/Shtterstock, p. 18; Sashatigar/iStock/Thinkstock (doodle art on contents page and fact boxes); Uppercut Images/Uppercut Images/Getty Images, p. 23; Yagi Studio/Digital Vision/Getty Images, p. 6.

Cover Credits: Monkey Business Images/Shutterstock.com (group of kids); Purestock/Thinkstock (series logo); Shouoshu/iStock/Thinkstock (digital background).